Science Biographies

Neil Armstrong

Catherine Chambers

Raintree is an imprint of Capstone Global Library Limited, a company incorporated in England and Wales having its registered office at 7 Pilgrim Street, London, EC4V 6LB – Registered company number: 6695582

www.raintreepublishers.co.uk
myorders@raintreepublishers.co.uk

Edited by Dan Nunn, Adam Miller, and Diyan Leake
Designed by Cynthia Akiyoshi
Picture research by Tracy Cummins
Production by Helen McCreath
Originated by Capstone Global Library Ltd
Printed and bound in China by CTPS

ISBN 978 1 406 27242 0
17 16 15 14 13
10 9 8 7 6 5 4 3 2 1

Chambers, Catherine
Neil Armstrong. (Science Biographies)
A full catalogue record for this book is available from the British Library.

Acknowledgements
We would like to thank the following for permission to reproduce photographs: Alamy pp. 5 (© interfoto), 9 (© David McGill), 10 (© BG Motorsports); AP Photo p. 12 (Associated Press); Corbis pp. 6 (© Corbis), 8 (© David Howells); Getty Images pp. 18 (Rolls Press/Popperfoto), 24 (Time Life Pictures/NASA), 28 (Jose Jordan/AFP); istockphoto p. 13 (Jason Titzer); NASA pp. 4 (Johnson Space Center Media Archive), 19, 20, 21, 22, 23, 25, 26, 27 (Bill Taub), design elements; Courtesy ot the Ohio Historical Society pp. 7, 17; Shutterstock p. 15 (© DeepGreen); design elements (© Dr_Flash, © Vacclav, © RoyStudio.eu, © David Woods); U.S. Air Force p. 14; U.S. Department of Defense p. 11; U.S. Navy p. 16 (Photo by Petty Officer 3rd Class Travis K. Mendoza).

Cover photograph of Neil Armstrong reproduced with permission of NASA and of the full moon reproduced with permission of Shutterstock (© Dundanim).

Every effort has been made to contact copyright holders of material reproduced in this book. Any omissions will be rectified in subsequent printings if notice is given to the publisher.

Contents

Some words are shown in **bold**, like this. You can find out what they mean by looking in the glossary.

Who was Neil Armstrong?

Imagine a world where the solar system was just a mystery through a telescope. Where the Moon was a ball of blue mountains and valleys. Passenger flights across the Atlantic Ocean were a new thrill. Jet aeroplanes were only just making their first trails in the skies.

Into this world was born the first man to step out onto the Moon. A man who was also a remarkable pilot, **aerospace** engineer, and astronaut. His name was Neil Alden Armstrong, and he was born on 5 August 1930.

This is Neil Armstrong inside the vehicle which landed on the Moon on 20 July 1969.

Seaplanes like this one took passengers across massive lakes in North America and Africa.

Neil started life in the country town of Wapakoneta, Ohio, in the United States. His parents were Stephen and Viola Armstrong. Neil had a sister, June, and a brother, Dean. Neil got the qualities of "inventiveness, concentration, organization, and perseverance" from his mother. He got his passion for aeroplanes from his father.

Top technology

Seaplanes that could land on water were developed in the 1930s. Massive rocket-shaped balloons called **Zeppelins** took tourists across the seas. But pilots had to wait for new jet technology before they could fly at high **altitudes**.

In awe of the aeroplane

What inspired Neil to take to the air? His father took him to the Cleveland Air Race at the age of just two. Neil also enjoyed playing with a tin toy aeroplane that his mother bought for him. At the age of six, he went on his first flight, in a Ford Trimotor plane. His brother Dean recalled that this was the most important early experience of Neil's life.

The Tin Goose

The Ford Trimotor was built in 1927 as one of the first all-metal planes. It was nicknamed the "Tin Goose". The plane's three engines took it higher and faster than others of the time. In 1929, the Norwegian pilot Berndt Balehen (1899–1973) flew it over the South Pole.

Neil himself said his deep interest in flight grew from the age of eight or nine. He spent hours making model aeroplanes. More than this, he drew designs never seen before, with retractable landing gear. That is where the wheels pull up under the aeroplane's belly at take-off. With this incredible imagination, it is no surprise that Neil wanted to be a designer, not a pilot!

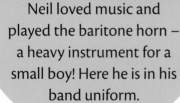

Neil loved music and played the baritone horn – a heavy instrument for a small boy! Here he is in his band uniform.

Up, up, and away!

Neil's father was an **auditor** for the state of Ohio. The job meant that he travelled a lot with his family, checking how the state spent its money. The Armstrongs had to move house 20 times!

When Neil was 14, the family returned to Wapakoneta, and Neil settled down well at Blume High School. He joined the Scout movement and was encouraged to explore. This love of exploring his own country and beyond never left him.

Wapakoneta's Armstrong Air & Space Museum displays Neil's flying history.

ARMSTRONG
AIR & SPACE MUSEUM

First flight

At just 15, Neil and his friends took flying lessons at an airfield in Wapakoneta. The lessons were expensive, so Neil worked in a chemist's shop for 40 cents an hour to pay for them. He passed his test on his 16th birthday and took his **first solo flight** just a week later!

First aircraft

At Wapakoneta, there were old World War II planes and training craft such as the Vultee BT-13 and the Fairchild PT-19. There was also the new Aeronca Chief training aircraft. Neil flew this basic Aeronca model called Champ (above). The pilot's seat is at the front and raised above a dipped nose for good visibility.

Designs for the skies

Neil applied to university to study aerospace engineering, following his true passion. He wanted the US Navy to help pay for his course. So, aged just 16, Neil calmly flew 480 kilometres (300 miles) to register for the US Navy scholarship-qualifying exam!

Neil enrolled at Purdue University, Indiana, in 1947. He gained the Holloway Plan naval scholarship, too. On the Plan, Neil had to study for two years, serve three in the US Navy, and study for two more.

Neil joined Purdue Airport's Avionics Club in his spare time. He worked on planes like this 1940s Boeing Stearman PT-17 Kaydet.

A FULL COURSE

Neil studied some very serious maths, together with engineering drawing, **welding**, and the behaviour of hot metals. Studying and getting fit on the physical education programme filled Neil's days.

Breaking records

On 14 October 1947, Captain Charles "Chuck" Yeager broke the **sound barrier** in the rocket-powered Bell X-1. Neil admired the Bell X-1 but was sad to see the end of records achieved through older **propeller planes**. His heroes were pioneer pilots such as Charles Lindbergh and Amelia Earhart.

In this photograph, Chuck Yeager is standing by the side of the Bell X-1. He named it *Glamorous Glennis* after his wife!

GLAMOROUS GLENNIS

War above the clouds

In 1949, Armstrong left Purdue for three years to train at Pensacola Naval Air Station. He gained his Naval Aviator **wings** in 1950. By then, the United States was at war with Korea. But Armstrong did not take part until 1951.

Armstrong often flew alongside his commanding officer, Marshall Beebe. They flew extremely fast F9F-2 Panthers. The days of the slow Aeronca Champ were a happy but distant memory.

The crowds cheered as Armstrong's aircraft carrier returned to the United States in 1952.

No fear of flying

Armstrong survived a close shave while landing his aircraft on the deck of an aircraft carrier. Another time, his plane was hit by enemy gunfire and struck a tall pole. Armstrong had to bail out. Was he put off? Never!

Returning to learning

Armstrong was 22 when he returned to Purdue University. He was confident after his navy experiences and graduated with a good degree in 1955. Armstrong became truly content when he became engaged to another Purdue student, Janet Shearon.

Armstrong gained both knowledge and practical experience at Purdue University.

In the fast lane

The United States' National Advisory Committee for Aeronautics (NACA) was forging ahead with superfast **jet propulsion**. After leaving Purdue, Armstrong was keen to be a test pilot at their High-Speed Flight Station (H-SFS) at Edwards Air Force Base in California.

DISAPPOINTMENT — THEN DELIGHT

There were no openings at H-SFS but Armstrong's application was sent on to Lewis Flight Propulsion Laboratory in Cleveland, Ohio. They wanted him!

At Lewis, Armstrong and fellow crew member Joseph Algranti flew this P-82 aircraft. It had a test rocket that was launched from underneath its belly.

At Lewis, Armstrong worked as a scientist and engineer as much as a test pilot. He investigated anti-icing systems and the effects of heat on **supersonic** aircraft. As well as this, Armstrong designed components, analysed data, and drew many diagrams. He really got to know supersonic and space flight inside out.

The open road

Was Armstrong just a very serious, hard-working man? No, not a bit of it! He loved cars and travelling. In 1952, he bought an Oldsmobile 88, like the one in this picture. He toured from Mexico to Canada with his brother Dean.

Moving on up

Armstrong stayed at Lewis for only five months before he got his dream job. He became a test pilot for the NACA High-Speed Flight Station at Edwards Air Force Base. There, Armstrong tested X-15s, aircraft that flew at supersonic speeds, way above the speed of sound. He tested the aircrafts' performance and helped thrust forward supersonic and rocket science.

A cloud forms behind this FA-18 Hornet just as it breaks the sound barrier.

Armstrong's work led to a place on the Man In Space Soonest program in 1958. This was the same year that NACA became NASA, the National Aeronautics and Space Administration. The Man In Space Soonest program tested flight equipment for manned space. Armstrong was on his way up!

Armstrong married Janet Shearon in 1956. They had two sons. Their daughter died from cancer when she was only three.

Not all plain sailing

Armstrong's technical knowledge was greatly admired. But some criticized him as a pilot. Chuck Yeager thought he was too mechanical and lacked natural flair. Armstrong did have accidents at Edwards, but so did others. He really pushed limits, which made accidents more likely.

The chosen few

The USSR (now Russia) was the first country to send a man into space. Then on 25 May 1961, the US President, John F. Kennedy, made a promise. By 1970, his country would land a man on the Moon and return him safely to Earth.

On 12 April 1961, the Russian Yuri Gagarin became the first man in space.

At this time, the United States was well into its manned space programme, Project Mercury (1959–1963). On 5 May 1961, it launched its first man, Alan Shepard, into space.

What about Armstrong? In 1962, he became one of the "New Nine" astronauts assigned to the Gemini space programme. So far, Mercury had launched one man at a time. Gemini aimed to send two. Later, Apollo would send three – and aim for the Moon!

Armstrong had to pass desert survival training before he could go to the Moon.

Tested to the limits

Armstrong had to go through many tests to see if he was fit for space travel and its extreme temperatures. His ears were syringed with iced water and his feet were plunged in it! He sat in heat of 63 degrees Celsius (145 degrees Fahrenheit). But he had fun wearing a spacesuit in the **weightlessness simulator**!

A spin in space

Armstrong approached *Agena* very slowly as they docked, at about 8 centimetres (3 inches) per second.

At last! Armstrong was chosen as the **Command Pilot** on Gemini 8. His co-pilot was David Scott. Their mission was groundbreaking. They had to **dock**, or link up their spacecraft, with *Agena*, a **module** already in space. David Scott was to perform a space walk.

A CLOSE SHAVE

On 16 March 1966, they blasted off towards *Agena* and docked successfully. But the two spacecraft began to roll uncontrollably. Fuel was running out. Armstrong cut short the mission and pulled away from *Agena*. Still in a spin, he switched on the **Re-entry Control System**. The spinning stopped! Armstrong prepared for splashdown. Saved! But he was disappointed that David Scott's space walk never happened.

Cool, calm, and commanding

Armstrong had proved his worth. After Gemini 8, he was chosen as back-up Command Pilot for Gemini 11 – and then, for Apollo 8. Armstrong knew that after backing-up Apollo 8 he would fly Apollo 11 – the mission to the Moon! In fact, he was chosen to command it.

Apollo, here we come!

Neil Armstrong, Michael Collins, and Buzz Aldrin shot into space on 16 July 1969 from the Kennedy Space Center in Florida. In Houston, Texas, a huge team of space experts kept in contact with the astronauts. Nearly 600 million people watched on live television.

SM

CM

LM

Apollo 11 had the *Saturn V* Service Module (SM), *Columbia* Command Module (CM), and *Eagle* Lunar Module (LM).

Perfect partners

Like Armstrong, Michael Collins (born 1930) had been a test pilot at Edwards. He had orbited Earth 44 times on Gemini 10. Buzz Aldrin (born 1930) was also a top class pilot and space scientist. He flew on Gemini 12 and had spent many hours walking outside the spacecraft.

Collins piloted Apollo 11's *Saturn V* rocket, which launched the astronauts and space modules. It was so fast it seemed a little unstable. But the rocket circled Earth one-and-a-half times then steered towards the Moon.

Saturn V then fell away, and Collins piloted the *Columbia* module closer to the Moon's surface. Armstrong and Aldrin crawled into *Eagle*, the lunar module. *Eagle* separated from *Columbia* and on 20 July Armstrong and Aldrin began their Moon landing.

Lift-off! At 9.32 a.m., on 16 July 1969, the *Saturn V* rocket launched Apollo 11.

The first man on the Moon

Armstrong took *Eagle*'s controls. They were not on target. All Armstrong could see was boulders and clouds of dust. He looked ahead at a smoother spot and made a gentle touchdown.

Armstrong contacted Ground Control. "Houston! Tranquility Base here. The *Eagle* has landed." For 6½ hours, Armstrong and Aldrin checked out *Eagle* and their moon-walking equipment. It was time to open the hatch.

"One small step ..."

As he stepped on to the Moon, Armstrong said: "That's one small step for a man, one giant leap for mankind." He took photos, set up a television link, and planted the US flag. Aldrin joined him. They spent 2½ hours taking soil samples and more photos. Then it was time to rejoin *Columbia*.

A real leader

Aldrin said of Armstrong, "He got me there and he got me back. I made a couple of mistakes and fortunately they weren't that crucial!" Armstrong also took the best rock and soil samples of any Moon walker.

25

After Apollo

For three weeks, Armstrong and his team were **quarantined**, or kept well away from other people. This was in case they had a space disease!

Armstrong had fun playing the ukulele while in quarantine!

Then, in open-top cars, they paraded through the streets of New York, Chicago, and Los Angeles – all in one day! The team toured 24 countries and 27 cities in 45 days, shaking hands with the world.

Armstrong was a great ambassador, but he found fame hard to handle. The pressure led to the end of his marriage with Janet. In 1994, Armstrong found happiness again when he married Carol Knight.

STILL A BUSY LIFE

Armstrong became NASA's Deputy Associate Administrator and held this position until 1971. For eight years after that, he was Professor of Aerospace Engineering at the University of Cincinnati. He also gave advice to science and technology businesses.

Armstrong loved meeting people but he soon hated the media spotlight.

Mission complete

Apollo missions to the Moon ended in 1972, after six landings on the Moon. After that, NASA aimed further, even to Mars, where robots, not humans, carry out experiments.

Remembering Armstrong

Even towards the end of his life, Armstrong said he dreamed of flying a manned mission to Mars!

Armstrong had a heart operation on 7 August 2012. Sadly, there were complications following the operation. Armstrong died on 25 August.

Armstrong posed at age 75 in front of a photo of his younger self. When Armstrong died, seven years later, US President Barack Obama called him a national hero.

"Think of Neil Armstrong"

At his death, Armstrong's family together made this plea: "Honour his example of service, accomplishment, and modesty, and the next time you walk outside on a clear night and see the Moon smiling down at you, think of Neil Armstrong and give him a wink."

Timeline

1930   Neil Alden Armstrong is born in Wapakoneta, Ohio, USA, on 5 August

1936   Flies for the first time, in a Ford Trimotor Plane at the Cleveland Air Race

1938   Starts to make model aeroplanes and aeroplane designs

1945   Takes flying lessons at the airfield in Wapakoneta

1946   Passes his flying exams and gets his pilot's licence at just 16 years of age

1947   Enrols at Purdue University, Indiana, to study aerospace engineering; receives a scholarship from the US Navy

1949   Interrupts his studies to serve three years in the US Navy, which is a condition of his scholarship

1950   Gains his Naval Aviator wings

1951   Serves in the Korean War

1952   Returns to Purdue University

1955   Gets his degree; works as a flight scientist and engineer at Lewis Flight Propulsion Laboratory; moves to Edwards Air Force Base where he flies at supersonic speed

1956   Marries Janet Shearon

1958   Is selected for the NASA Man In Space Soonest program to train for space flight; continues to work as a scientist and engineer

1961   The Russian Yuri Gagarin becomes the first man in space. US President John Kennedy promises that America would land a man on the Moon before 1970.

1962   Armstrong becomes one of the "New Nine" astronauts on the Gemini manned space programme

1966   Armstrong and David Scott pilot the *Gemini 8* mission to dock with a module in space

1969   Armstrong is chosen to command Apollo 11. On 20 July, Armstrong, Buzz Aldrin, and Michael Collins reach the Moon, where Armstrong takes the first human step.

1971   Returns to space science and engineering; leaves NASA and spends the rest of his life as a teacher, researcher, and technology business advisor

2012   Neil Alden Armstrong dies on 25 August

Glossary

aerospace Earth's atmosphere and space beyond it

altitude height, especially above Earth

auditor person who examines money accounts

Command Pilot pilot in charge of a mission

dock link up with another module in space

first solo flight pilot's first flight on their own after passing flying exams

jet propulsion jet of gas rushing backwards that shoots a rocket or aeroplane forward

module small pod built for astronauts to fly in or to take equipment into space

propeller plane aeroplane that moves forward when engines turn propellers

quarantined when a person is shut away from other people to prevent the spread of disease

Re-entry Control System control system designed to help a spacecraft re-enter Earth's atmosphere

seaplane aeroplane with smooth runners that enable it to land on water

sound barrier speed-of-sound point that is difficult for aircraft to pass

supersonic travelling faster than the speed of sound

weightlessness simulator machine made to copy the weightless conditions found in space so that astronauts can practise moving in them

welding joining two pieces of metal by melting their edges and pressing on them to make a solid joint

wings badge gained when a pilot passes the flying test

Zeppelin massive gas-filled balloon that flies people in a carriage attached underneath

Find out more

BOOKS

Space (Explorer Tales), Nick Hunter (Raintree, 2012)

Spacebusters: The Race to the Moon, Philip Wilkinson (Dorling Kindersley, 2012)

Who Was Neil Armstrong?, Roberta Edwards (Puffin Books, 2012)

WEBSITE

www.bbc.co.uk/science/space/solarsystem/astronauts
You can find lots of information about space on the BBC website, including video of the Moon landing.

PLACES TO VISIT

Science Museum
South Kensington, London SW7 2DD
www.sciencemuseum.org.uk/visitmuseum/galleries/space.aspx
Explore our galaxy and get close up to replica rockets, satellites, space probes, and landers.

National Space Centre
Exploration Drive, Leicester LE4 5NS
www.spacecentre.co.uk
This has so much – a planetarium plus galleries of rockets, space suits, meteorites, and even videoconference sessions with astronauts such as Timothy Peake.

Glasgow Science Centre
50 Pacific Way, Glasgow GS1 1EA
www.gsc.org.uk
This has a great planetarium and you can learn a lot in the stargazer sessions.

Index